PUSHES AND PULLS

By

Steffi Cavell-Clarke

©2017
Book Life
King's Lynn
Norfolk PE30 4LS

ISBN: 978-1-78637-106-5

All rights reserved
Printed in Malaysia

Written by:
Steffi Cavell-Clarke

Edited by:
Grace Jones

Designed by:
Danielle Jones

A catalogue record for this book
is available from the British Library

PHOTO CREDITS

**Abbreviations: l-left, r-right, b-bottom,
t-top, c-centre, m-middle.**

Front cover – Pressmaster. 2 – Sergey Novikov. 4 – Brian A Jackson. 5– Tom Wang. 6 – Valua Vitaly. 7 – . 8 – Jorge Casais. 9 –Veronica Louro. 10 – sainthorantdaniel. 11 – Jim Lopes. 12 – Hatchapong Palurtchaivong. 13 – colors. 14 –Nataliia Zhekova. 15 – Pressmaster. 16 – DnDavis. 17 – Halfpoint. 18 – Sergei Kolesnikov. 19 –TairA. 20 – MarcusVDT. 21 – janecocoa. 22l&r – Lucie Lang 22m – My_inspiration. 23tl – Narintorn_m2 23bl – John99 23tr – Ledimup 23br – oksana2-10.
Images are courtesy of Shutterstock.com.
With thanks to Getty Images, Thinkstock Photo and iStockphoto.

CONTENTS

Words that look like this can be found in the glossary on page 24.

What is SCIENCE?

What does a force do?

What's the difference between a push and a pull?

What makes things move?

Science can answer many difficult questions we may have and help us to understand the world around us.

What is a FORCE?

A force makes something move. You cannot see a force but you can see and feel its effects.

Pushes and pulls are two different types of force.

How Do You
PUSH and PULL

Push

You can push trollies in a supermarket.

You use your body to push things away from you.
You usually push things to make them move forward.

You can also use your body to pull objects towards you.

Each team is pulling the rope towards them.

Pull

Pull

Natural FORCES

There are natural forces which can push and pull too. Wind is a natural force.

Wind moves air. You can see its effect as it pushes through the trees.

Changing
SHAPE

Push and pull forces can change the shape of things by squashing, stretching or bending them.

You can push or pull soft clay to make many different shapes.

Changing DIRECTION

Pushes and pulls can change the direction of a moving object.

Footballers use their feet to push a football.
They can push the football in different directions.

Changing SPEED

Pushes and pulls can make an object move faster or slower. The harder an object is pushed, the faster and further it will travel.

16

A pull can be used to slow down an object that is moving in the opposite direction.

17

STOPPING

Pushing or pulling against a moving object can make it stop.

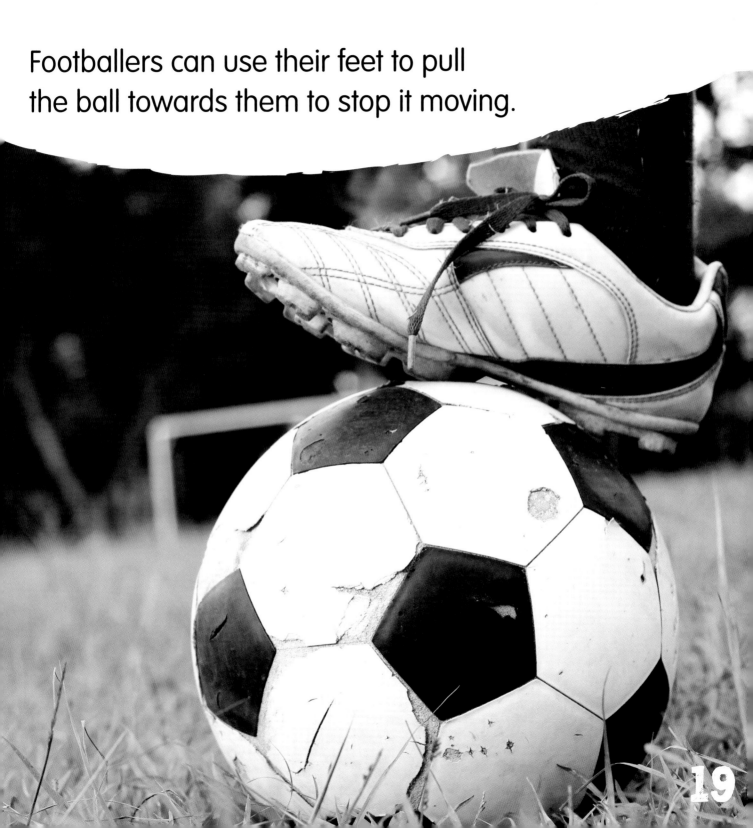

Footballers can use their feet to pull the ball towards them to stop it moving.

19

GRAVITY

Gravity is a force that pulls everything down towards the ground.

You are able to see the effects of gravity when you let go of an object, because it falls to the ground.

Let's
EXPERIMENT!

How can we use a force to change the shape of an object? Let's find out!

YOU WILL NEED:

Blue clay
Red clay
Yellow clay
A clean surface

STEP 1

Place the blue clay onto a clean surface.
Use your hands to push the clay over onto a table and then roll it between your hand and the table.

STEP 2

Pick up the red clay. Use your hands to push and roll the clay into a round ball.

22

Now pick up the yellow clay and pull it apart to make smaller pieces.

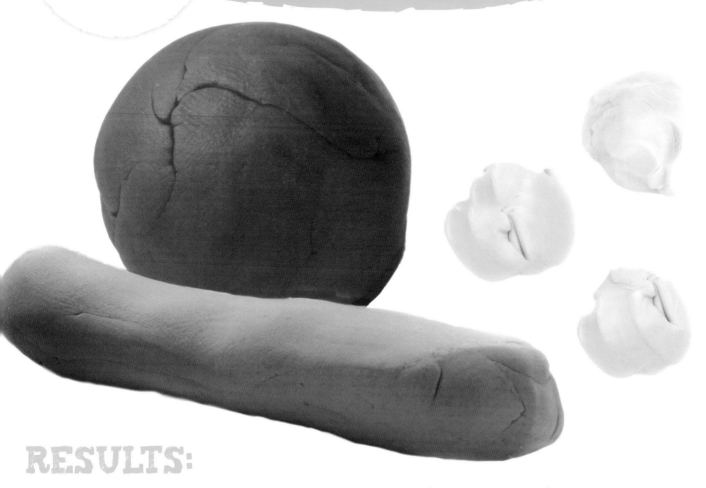

RESULTS:

Look at the different shapes you have made. This shows you how pushes and pulls can change the shape of objects.

GLOSSARY

clay	a natural material used to make things
direction	the way something is moving
effects	the results of something
natural	something made by nature, not by people or machines
objects	things that can be seen and touched

INDEX